hc

This DangerSpot book belongs to:

Published in 2005 by DangerSpot Books Ltd.
Old Bank House,
High Street,
Laxfield,
Woodbridge,
Suffolk.
IP13 8DX.
www.dangerspot.co.uk

Printed by Proost NV, Turnhout, Belgium.

ISBN 0-9546565-4-7

The Dangerous Road Game

Hedley Griffin

DangerSpot Books Ltd.

It was a warm, goal-scoring day when everything in the world seemed sporty. Harey, the hare-brained rabbit, lay on his bed dreaming of being the best football player in the world.

'I bet I will score more goals than the captain of England,' he boasted, as he rushed to put on his football boots, but he was in too much of a hurry to do up his bootlaces.

He grabbed his football, rushed out of the bedroom, tripped over his untied laces and fell down the stairs.

'Oh! Argh! Ouch!' he yelled as he landed at the bottom.

'Are you alright?' asked Scampi the cat and Chips the dog

when they saw Harey lying on the floor in the hall.

'Your bootlaces are undone, Harey. That's why you tripped up coming down the stairs,' scolded Scampi.

'Tie your laces! Tie your laces!' repeated Pillow the parrot.

'Do you want to play football in the park?' asked Harey.

'Yeah!' said Chips. 'Can I be in goal?'

'You bet,' said Harey, gathering his football and racing to the door.

'Come on. Hurry up. You're wasting time.'

He backed out on to the pavement without looking where he was going, bumped into a large snail and tripped over.

'Why don't you look where you're going?' moaned Harey at the snail.
'You're always rushing around, bumping into things.'

'You should look where you're going!' said the surprised snail.

'Yes, Harey. Why don't you look where you're going?' repeated Pillow the parrot.

'I'm off to play football. Are you coming?' said Harey,
as he turned around and ran smack into a lamp-post.

'Argh! Oh! My nose! It hurts! Somebody put that lamp-post in the way!' screamed Harey.

'Harey, you must look where you're going,' advised Scampi, as she took his hand. 'Let's cross over the road to the park further along where we can see in all directions. It would be safer there. The road here is on a bend and just before the top of the hill.'

'We'll be over the hill and round the bend!' laughed Pillow.

'We must stop, look and listen,' advised Scampi,

holding Harey and Chips by the hand.

She then noticed Harey and Pillow were standing on the edge of the pavement.

'You and Pillow should stand back from the edge!' she said.

'Stand back from the edge of the pavement. Stand well back!' repeated Pillow, while he and Harey moved backwards from the edge of the kerb.

'Can we cross now?' said Harey, who was always in a hurry.

'No, not yet. We must give ourselves plenty of time to look around and listen.
We must look in every direction, and if it's all clear we can cross,' said Scampi.

'Oh yes,' said Chips, thoughtfully. 'Look up, look down, and then look back again, and if it's a nice, clear day we can cross. Is that right?'

'Oh dear,' said Scampi. 'I forgot. Dogs don't have any road sense. Just hold my hand and we'll cross together.'

When they saw the road was clear and it was safe to cross they walked over towards the park. Harey tried to run ahead.

'No, Harey! You mustn't run across. That is dangerous. You must always walk, never run,' said Scampi.

'Walk the walk,' repeated Pillow.

'Look at me. I always walk everywhere. I never fly.'

'That's because you're afraid of heights,' laughed Scampi,
and Pillow blushed.

In the park, Harey tackled Scampi, and Chips tackled Harey,
while Pillow played the referee.

'And the captain of England gets the ball and tackles the defence, cleverly dribbles around his opponent, lines up the goal, and scores! Hooray!'

Harey kicked the ball so hard it bounced into the road.

'I'll get it,' shouted Harey, racing after the ball.

'Come back! You're offside! You're offside!' yelled Pillow,
who did not really understand what it meant.

Harey ran into the road without looking.
'No! Don't!' shrieked Scampi,
running to the edge of the pavement,
but she was too late.
'Look out!'

Suddenly, there was a screech of brakes and a loud 'bumpf'.

Harey had been hit by a passing car.

Harey was taken to hospital. Fortunately, the car had been going very slowly and he was not too severely hurt, but he did have to stay in hospital for two weeks and could not go out to play. He would always stop, look, and listen before crossing the road in future.

Place the DangerSpot stickers around your home as a reminder of the dangers and keep your children safe!

The **Green Cross Code** is a guide for everyone
showing how to cross the road safely.

1. Think first.
Find the safest place to cross then stop.
If possible cross the road at:
subways, footbridges, islands, Zebra, Pelican and **traffic light crossings** or where there is a **police officer, school crossing patrol** or **traffic warden**. If you can't find any good crossing places like these, choose a place where you can see clearly along the roads in all directions, and where drivers can see you.
Never cross on sharp bends or just before the top of a hill.

2. Stop
Stand on the pavement near the kerb.
Give your self lots of time to **have a good look all round.**
Stand a little way back from the kerb - where you will be away from traffic, but where you can still see if anything is coming.
If there is no pavement, stand back from the edge of the road but where you can still see traffic coming.

3. Use your eyes and ears.
Look all around for traffic, and listen.
Look in every direction. Listen carefully because you can sometimes hear traffic before you can see it.

4 .Wait until it's safe to cross.
If traffic is coming, let it pass.
Do not cross unless there is a safe gap and you are sure there is plenty of time.
If you are not sure, don't cross.

5. Look and listen.
When it's safe, walk straight across the road.
Always walk across, **never run**.

6. Arrive alive.
Keep looking and listening for traffic while you cross.

Supporting the THINK! road safety campaign